Letter Tracing Carter's Way

BOOK FOR PRESCHOOL & KINDERGARTEN

By Iman Drummond, Author of "Carter's Way: All the Things You Can Be"

Copyright © 2022 by Iman N. Drummond

All rights reserved. No part of this book may be reproduced or copied in any manner without written permission from the author. For more information, contact:
booksbyiman@gmail.com
www.booksbyiman.com

ISBN: 978-0-578-36310-3

A a

Artist   artist

A A A   a a a

Artist

artist

B b

Beekeeper   beekeeper

B   B   B   b   b   b

Beekeeper

beekeeper

C c

Coach   coach

C C C c c c

Coach

coach

D d

Dentist   dentist

D D D   d d d

Dentist

dentist

Engineer engineer

E E E   e e e

Engineer

engineer

F f

Firefighter firefighter

F F F f f f

Firefighter

firefighter

G g

Gardener gardener

G G G g g g

Gardener

gardener

Hairstylist   hairstylist

H H H   h h h

Hairstylist

hairstylist

I i

Icecream Man   icecream man

I I I   i i i

Icecream Man

icecream man

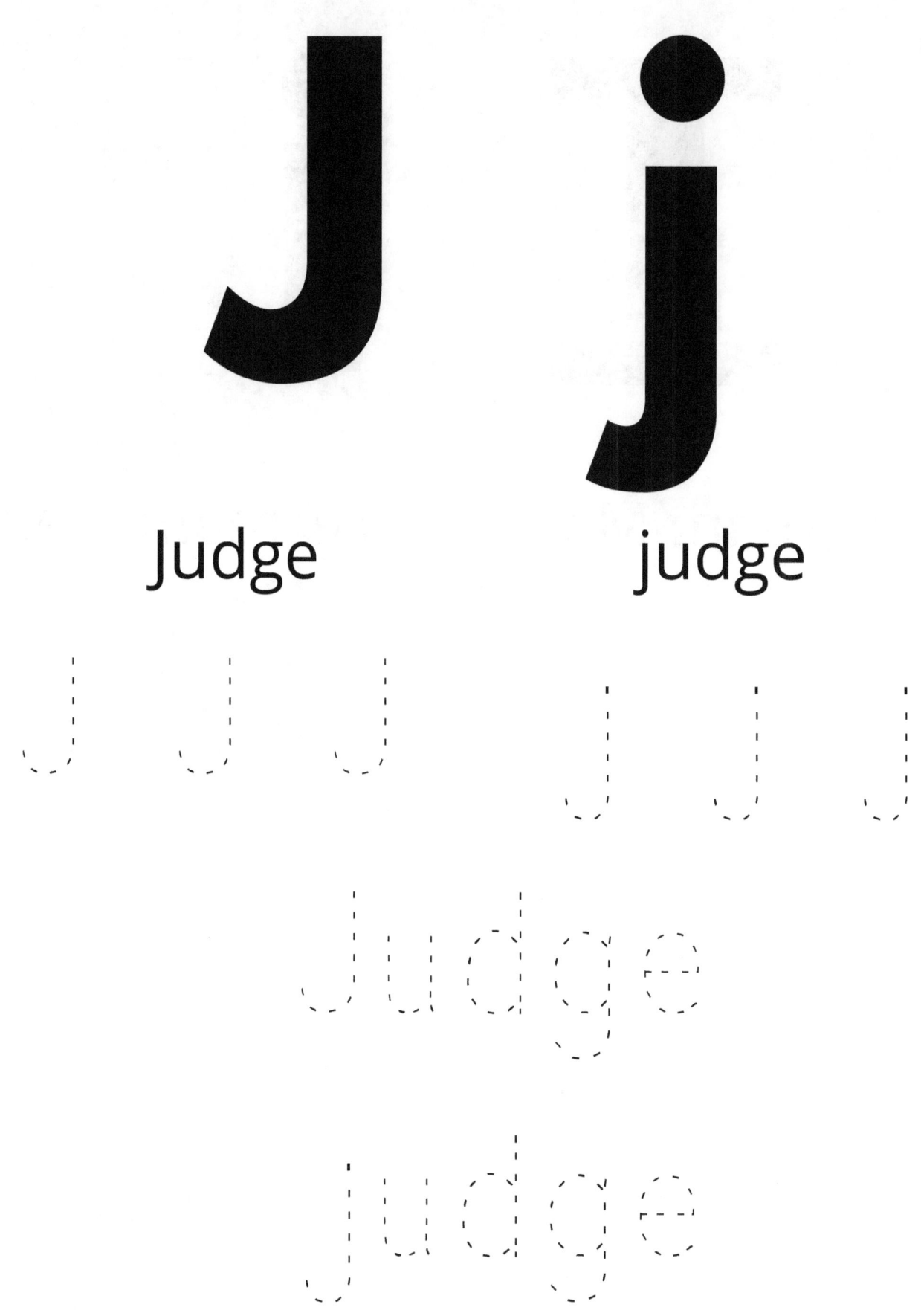

K k
Karate Teacher   karate teacher

K K K   k k k

Karate Teacher

karate teacher

L l

Librarian   librarian

L L L   l l l

Librarian

librarian

Musician   musician

M   M   M   M   m   m   m

Musician

musician

N n

Nurse   nurse

N N N   n n n

Nurse

nurse

Optometrist   optometrist

O O O   o o o

Optometrist

optometrist

P p

Pilot pilot

P P P p p p

Pilot

pilot

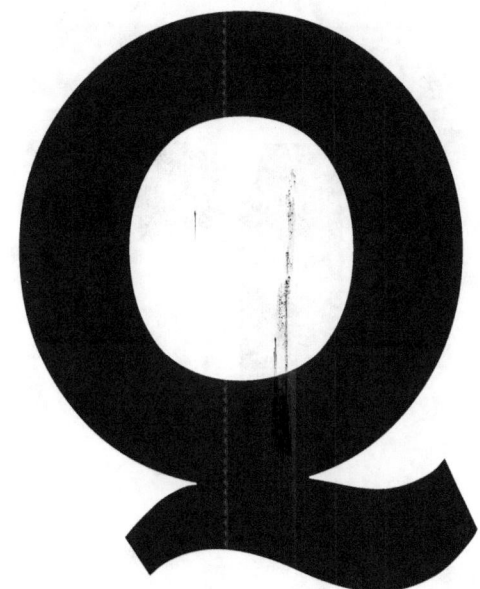 

Quilter   quilter

Q Q Q   q q q

Quilter

quilter

R r

Racecar Driver   racecar driver

R R R   r r r

Racecar Driver

racecar driver

S s

Scientist   scientist

S S S   s s s

Scientist

scientist

Teacher	teacher

T T T		t t t

Teacher

teacher

Umpire   umpire

U U U   u u u

Umpire

umpire

Veterinarian   veterinarian

v v v   v v v

Veterinarian

veterinarian

W w

Writer writer

W w W w W w W w

Writer

writer

X-Ray Technician

x-ray technician

X X X   x x x

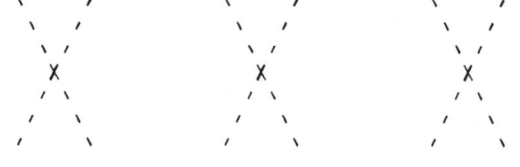

Yachtsman   yachtsman

Y Y Y Y y y y y

Yachtsman

yachtsman

Z z

Zookeeper   zookeeper

Z Z Z   z z z

Zookeeper

zookeeper

www.ingramcontent.com/pod-product-compliance
Lightning Source LLC
Chambersburg PA
CBHW082337300426
44109CB00045B/2471